What Happens Next Is Anyone's Guess

ALSO BY CAROL POTTER

Some Slow Bees (Oberlin College Press, 2015)

Otherwise Obedient (Red Hen Press, 2007)

Short History of Pets (Cleveland State University Poetry Center, 2000)

Upside Down in the Dark (Alice James Books, 1995)

Before We Were Born (Alice James Books, 1990)

WHAT HAPPENS NEXT
IS ANYONE'S GUESS

Poems

Carol Potter

Pacific Coast Poetry Series

An imprint of BEYOND BAROQUE BOOKS

What Happens Next Is Anyone's Guess

This book was published with the aid of a grant from
The Lawrence Lipton Trust

Pacific Coast Poetry Series
An imprint of Beyond Baroque Books
ISBN: 978-1-892184-27-6

Cover Design
Ash Goodwin

Cover Art
Sea
by Koga Harue

Beyond Baroque Literary/Arts Center

681 Venice Boulevard
Venice, CA, 90291

310-822-3006
www.beyondbaroque.org

Pacific Coast Poetry Series

Acknowledgements

Agni: "Ode to Smoke"
Blue Line: "Mercy"
Field: "Déjà-vu, or How We Got Out of the Swamp"; "A Common Misperception"; "When we brought the anaconda"
Frontier: "Are You Going to Eat That?; "What Month Is This, What Year?"
Green Mountains Review: "Thanks for the Coke"; "There Being No Puppies"; "Good Pink, Bad Pink"; "What Moves"; "Never Say You're Sorry"
Hanging Loose: "Seven Girls Driving Around Town"
Hayden's Ferry: "Replacement"
Hotel Amerika: "On a Scale of 1-10, 10 Being the Most Satisfied"; "Most Know Better"; "I know it was not nice of me"
The Kenyon Review: "Nothing But Blue Skies"
The Los Angeles Review: "Stealth, or a Sweet Bit of Stealing"; "Walking the Ice"
The Massachusetts Review: "Musac"
Naugatuck River Review: "Kettle Pond"
New England Review: "The Good Dark"
On the Seawall: "Heaven's Breath"
Plume: "Lion Cub" ("We'd taken to being clever"); "Whales" ("When the whales washed")
Poet Lore: "One with Others"
Rattle: "Some Men in Plastic Cuffs" published as "In Which I Get Out of a Speeding Ticket"
River Styx: "Details and Procedures"
Roads Taken: Contemporary Vermont Poetry: "Bear Hunting in North America; "What Moves"
The Laurel Review: "The Requisite Bad Hair"
UnBroken Journal: "When the archeologists"; "I didn't know her raising rats" ("Tickled Pink")
Valparaiso: "Nightcrawlers" ("He was outside digging")

With tremendous gratitude for the ongoing support, rigorous feedback, laughter and tears to the gals in my beloved po-group: Annie Boutelle, Amy Dryansky, Diana Gordon, Maya Janson, Mary Koncel, Ellen Doré Watson. And special thanks for Maureen Conroy and Tekla McInerney for helping me be there—for your early readings of my work and for always expanding my sense of possibilities—your friendship, humor, hospitality, and artistic selves. And with thanks and much gratitude to Beyond Baroque. Much gratitude for the honor of this prize, and to my editors, Suzanne Lummis and Liz Camfiord.

... The second time
The optics jibed. We saw to the edge of all there is—

So brutal and alive it seemed to comprehend us back.

—Tracy K. Smith, from "My God, It's Full of Stars"

For my family: my siblings & my daughters—with me from the start
—and for Zoey & Theo moving forward.

Contents

I: Replacement

II: Pernath's Hat

III. It Was Out There the Whole Time

IV: How We Came Up Out of the Swamp

I

Replacement

Thanks for the Coke

I was looking for you and I took a swim in your pool.
   It wasn't your pool. You never had a pool. It's the house

I grew up in. The pool is new. The people are new.
   It was a hot night in July. No one was home. I opened the gate,

took off my clothes, dove in, swam end to end.
   Thanks for the beer you left poolside. Thanks for the coke.

The barn across the road is broken and the cows wandering
   some road no one ever figured out.

Is that north? South? What next someone might ask.
   I was looking for you and I go on looking. That kitchen.

Those windows. How does any one person be that much gone?
   There it is, the full moon—so cold tonight it's like the moon

is a hole in the sky through which all heat goes. And the light
   on the snow, you could read by it. You could walk on it—

which apparently you did. The crust on top must have
   held you up. Must have made it possible to go where you went.

In daylight, I'll look for tracks. To see what came through
   while I slept. Where anything went.

What Moves

What moves might eat you or save you. Might be
    what you were looking for all along or what was looking for you
the whole day. What moves. The leaves on the trees. The dog
    across the field, then rolling in something dead. To keep it. Mark
it. Let anyone coming along behind him know it was his. Then later
    finding a skull and chewing on it. The dog as grave-digger.
As place-keeper. Sound asleep when the coyotes put up their yell
    from that crack in the earth coyotes call from. What moves
will be something alive. Is alive. Is the water tumbling
    through the trees and you need the water. Your own mother
diving into it wherever she could find it. You learned to drink.
    You drank from her though she sat quite still while you did it.
What moves is what you need. The sky spackled at the top
    of the hill. The wind that came blowing down. The sky.
That wind poking at the house. What moves might eat you or save you.
    The water you dove into to grab your mother who had dived into
something much too shallow to be diving into. The water your
    mother's mother dove into to pull the child from the water
though it was too late. How still that child was in your grandmother's
    arms. How still your mother was when she was watching it.
Your grandmother laying the child down in the sand. How the water
    kept on moving like nothing had happened. How the sky kept on
moving. How the breath moved in and out of all the people's lungs
    come to see the child lying still on the sand. How still your mother
was when she left you. When she pulled that last breath out of the room.
    How what moves might save you or eat you. How
quiet. How like the sea would be if it stopped. How stopped.
    How quiet. What saves us. What eats us.

Mercy

...it was nevertheless blank where a past did not haunt nor a future beckon...
—Toni Morrison

It is not a good idea to go there just to see what it is,
   or what might be next. Your future is separate and
anyone's guess except the one thing. Perhaps I am

blotting out how I came to be here this close to Canada
   walking my dog in the dark, after work. Ten degrees above
zero. Past the city rink where three boys skate beneath lights,

PA system blasting Norah Jones, *Don't know why I didn't call*,
   speaker nailed to a pole above the ice, and the voice laconic,
feeling empty as a drum. The boys crack into each other,

puck thudding against the fence, myself and the dog
   walking past. We'd been out on the lake. Watched the sun
go down until the cold got too cold. Listened to the sounds ice

makes, water contracting beneath the surface making a sort of
   tympanic sound. As if something were down there trying to bang
its way out. A certain rapture to it. Out that far, that late. Ice fishing shacks

lit up, people driving from one shore to another on their snow machines,
   some trucks, random cars. As if we had all discovered territory
nobody could claim. That kind of happiness. You can develop a taste

for it. As a teenager sometimes riding the horse too far too late,
   I'd come back in the dark, hands and feet numb from the cold.
What was it in me liked seeing the windows of the house lit up across

the field, my mother, sister, father already sitting down to dinner?
   Something satisfying in it. Something close to ruin. Feet too cold to stand.
Fingers half-frozen. I could barely un-hook the bridle.

On a Scale of 1-10, 10 Being the Most Satisfied

When I got there, the party was set to go
    but the host was getting irritable. Banging

plates; muttering under her breath,
    cursing. There was a pony in the room

cozying up to the table like this was where
    it was ordinarily fed. The pony kept

looking at me like I knew what to do.
    I was the guest of honor though for what

I wasn't altogether sure. It's a common
    occurrence for me. Most of the chairs

were empty but for two sleeping strangers
    just off the street. I wanted to shake them

by the shoulders but it seemed a shame
    to wake them. The Queen of the place

kept looking at me like she'd never seen
    me before and she hadn't. *Who are you?*

she asked. *What are you doing here?*
    I told her the story with a couple jokes

popped in but she was implacable.
    The party plans kept changing minute

by minute. A man with a name tag pinned
    to his plaid shirt and a hopeful look

on his face came in with a survey for me
    to fill out. *How would you rate this meal*

on a scale of 1-10? My breath failed me.
    Madame stomped from the table.

Fill it out, she said *Make sure you follow
    the goddamned directions.*

The survey was illegible. A script I could
    have read if I'd remembered my glasses.

If I'd been thinking before I left home.
    If I hadn't left home. If I'd ever been thinking.

Seven Girls Driving Around Town

If you got free by any strange behavior, they
    would have got there the other day leaning out the windows
driving around town, shouting something out now and again.
    Someone was singing softly in the backseat, but the driver wasn't sure

which one it was so many were packed in, and when
    they drove past a smoking woman waiting for a bus outside
the Family Dollar store, they slunk down in their seats because
    she was one of their mothers or might very well have been.

An hour or two had gone by and they were still
    driving about town, looking out at the lake, calling out to
people in the crosswalk, watching the freight train shuffle
    into town across the causeway and thinking about breaking the one

unbroken window in the abandoned discount store.
    They were aware there was some time going by that they could
have been doing other, more productive things like
    looking for new jobs for instance, maybe joining The Guard.

The driver was jerky. Speeding up, slowing down,
    turning in her seat chatting to the friends leaning out the windows.
they were exhausted when they got home, but excused themselves
    knowing as anyone knows it could always very well be the final day
of years of sweetness none the less.

One with Others

I was spending a day deciding to be happy. There was a wrong taxi
ride. I wasn't there. I was in line waiting to register. I was being
happy, humming something unidentifiable. I was being patient.
A woman in front of me had been waiting an hour. We were being ignored.
We were being nice. There was a war on but we weren't sure
which one it was. The sky lit up whether it was day or night.
Some delays here and there. People trying to put one thing
alongside another. This didn't fit with that and the other not with this.
There's the happiness we'd all decided on. That purpose. The class
in the sweet we go on eating. I was being one with others.
I was going along with the program. A woman said to me last night
that happiness is a matter of choice—some people choose to be happy,
others select a course that leads to frustration and disappointment.
You have to make a choice, she said, smiling at me.
I was being cooperative. I was trying to tell night from day
but the stars weren't out. I spent a day doing it. Trying to figure out
who was winning the war, and which happiness I had.
How I was laughing, and my lip was bleeding and no one
had been biting it.

Good Pink. Bad Pink.

When the child in mid-tantrum tried riding her pink scooter
   directly off the platform and onto the packed train at 28th
& Broadway, her un-brushed hair bunched up in the back, her pink
   jacket open, limbs flailing, we pretended to not see. Next to me
a man was leafing through the Sotheby's catalogue. Out the corner
   of my eye, I could see a Matisse I'd never seen before, then
Duchamp. The edges of the woman all in pieces. Cubed. Like the child
   in front of me. Hair, hands, eyeballs askew. Civilization
in its tweed coat on my left. The paintings he was studying
   but would not exactly share with me. I went back to minding
my own business but then mother took the scooter back from
   mad daughter who started twisting and screaming again.
I thought of telling her she could get arrested. Sent to reform school.
   Adopted out. Anything. Her older sister smiled at me beatifically,
as if to say, *look what I put up with*. She'd been dissembling,
   enjoying her sister's disintegration. Someone else the bad one.
Which I never got from my sister, nor her from me. That public tantrum.
   What we took apart we took apart quietly and in private.
Like that nude descending her staircase, one piece at a time; the steps
   not looking like steps. Just odd blocks.

Stealth, or a Sweet Bit of Stealing

She said she loved me. She was a mink stole.
A girl stole. The stole between her legs. Her breasts
stole me, her mouth had me. She and I stole from each
other. We drove to another state and the state
stole from us. Jesus stole something. There were signs
along the roadway: *Jesus Saves*. We were stealing
ourselves quietly by ourselves so no one could see.
There were cicadas stealing the silence from the air.
Stealing our words. Cracking them together between
their legs. We were stealing the state. We got stolen
from. There were bees in the apples stealing
sweet meat from the trees. There were apples on
the ground stealing dirt from the earth. There
were stealers stealing around us singing their bird
songs. There was a flood and a stealing stinging
bee sting. She stung me. I loved her. She stole and I stole
from her. She loved me. It was a sweet bit of stealing.
A nickel. A dime. A few years. Some bird song.

Mother May I?

We stepped on some cracks. We broke our mothers'
backs. We sold mother down the river. We are mother
fuckers. Mother of God. Mother of us all. The good
mother. Mother tongue. Mother country. Mommie
Dearest. You're not my mother. You sound just like
my mother. What would your mother say? Does your
mother know you're here? It'd break her heart. Your
mother. We've been looking for her. The Blessed Mother.
The Virgin Mother. We've hit the mother lode. Please
don't tell your mother. We thought it was her coming
down the road in the station wagon full of kids.
Those weren't our kids. That wasn't our wagon.
No, that's not your mother. If she could see you now.

A Brand No One Could Stand

Because she has that slit but still carries her tonsils
    like a daylily at the back of the throat, it would have

been better to have called a moratorium earlier, to have
    cancelled the garden. What can you do? A tad fearsome

she poled across the bubbling river. Mired in spring stems
    she emigrated into blooms, the red heads of

tulips bobbing; daffodils swaying in the breeze. There was a ban in progress.
    She had no idea where she was going. That root stirred in her.

She did not foresee the lone tails of cats, that rainy stint in a town
    where one's button could be undone. They say

we need carotene to grow, sunshine at the equinox. They say
    we need to do some begging; put up with the boss's ire.

She liked watching the sun on its pendulum oar its way
    into the day rocking itself open. She needed to know that particular

orchestration, but the responsibilities smacked of burlap and rot.
    It would have been idiotic to have fought that

registration, caused a riot though the language was
    indecipherable, and the macaroni at the company luncheon,

rancid. A brand no one could stand. However, the lake at the door
    was lovely, and the water tasted like ale.

Fishbowl

I knew I was done for when I heard the word
fishbowl from two different people in two different
conversations. That they were talking about where
I was working, the company's tight quarters.
My office was a small room with a window
at the top of it. If I cranked my head back, I could see
the sky and the top of a building. Beyond that building
there was a lake with mountains. If I stood on my desk,
put my head out the window, turned to the right,
I could see the water and the mountains of Canada.
I could see birds flying over the border.
Back, forth. Hopefully no one would come in
while I was standing on my desk or talking
on my cell phone. It could happen anytime and I
knew it. As the place was a fishbowl, as they said.
One bad word and the word got out.
In the neighboring office there was an actual
fishbowl. Sticky notes on all the surfaces except for
the fishbowl. One goldfish with its crenellated fins
waving. There were sucker fish in there too—
keeping the glass clean and the goldfish healthy.
You might be thinking this was not my 'bliss.'
That whispery place. That fishbowl. That fish.

Most Know Better

Orange yolk of a moon, and the fields gone dark. The animals, spooked, run back into their houses. Some of us kept walking into the cold to stare at the moon, but then the clouds came in. Somebody will have to tell me when the eclipse is done. Watch out! The gelding pummels the stall wall each time he puts his head into the trough. Four dogs stand at the glass door watching the ermine pick at the bird seed. On the other side of the wall we were making love. It was only fitting that the board your x left behind the bedroom door fell over and gave me a black eye. Sometimes the audience noise is too busy and there's no point. A spider dropped down in front of me. When I first arrived the horses gathered, nuzzled me. One chased my dog back through the gate. A dead porcupine means the end of innocence. Means it is snowing and it will go on snowing. Downstairs the x who came back and refuses to leave was cleaning the kitchen. You were playing your fiddle, leaning into the music with your eyes closed and did not hear me knocking. Since we're not young somebody will have to tell me when I lose. Someone once told me I was a thrasher and a blamer. In the book by your bed, the spider dropping down in front of a person means a man is looking out at the sea. Means a horse is running across a yard. Means there's a black eye in the making. There's some x's left over. Sometimes it looks like someone knows what she is doing. The dogs ran outside to chase the ermine. One horse stood on the front porch of the house. Down at the corner there's a Free sign next to a wooden chair filling up with snow. In the old days, some women wore ermine on the street, but now most know better.

Replacement

They brought my replacement in while
I was still in place. *Here's the desk you'll be
sitting in, here's the chair. This is the view. Here's
the pens and pencils.* I knew something
was going on exactly when something was going on.
I put my favorite pens and pencils off to the side
so the new person wouldn't ever touch them.
*These are the children in the picture frames you
will be seeing on your desk*, the supervisor said.
*Here's the screen and the keyboard. Here's the
hand sanitizer. This is where you put your boots.
Where you put snacks you shouldn't be eating.
Here you go.* I thought the new person replacing
me had a nice face. She was smiling. How we do
smile first day on the job. We smile and we nod
making sure everyone knows we'll be going along
with the program. My replacement shook my hand.
It's not every day you get to do that. Check out
your replacement. Give her the keys to the office.
Clean out the cup she'll be drinking from.
Show her where everything's kept.

Lost Cattle in the Forest

Some take to traveling. Leaving gates open. You might
forget to close the barn door. You might open the gate
when the horse runs for it. You might have seen the heifer
that escaped from the barnyard. You were a child then.
You knew nothing about going missing yet. Maybe something.
You knew the barn. The bank of lights in the field that looked
like an airplane. The cows at the windows strapped
in their stanchions, tails swinging. Your father heave-hoe-ing
udder to udder. The mythic first-calf heifer. It wasn't a
disaster, her calf born in the forest. Seen now and then
with the mother. The calf suckling for as long as the cow
would let her. All that milk in her mouth. Those farms they
skirted. On the lam. Disappeared. Living off the land.
Some saw the cow and the nearly grown calf outside the fence.
Some saw my brother. The forest. A flock of birds. You can
print it on you. Leaf mold. Twigs. A time. A place.
Since then, I've lost one horse. Two parents. A woman
I loved badly; a child that was never born. This is the call
cow and calf answered to when they reappeared bucked up
with burrs and under-weight. This is the stream they drank from.
What they did in the winter I have no idea.

Bear Hunting in North America

99 percent of my poems flew into the ether because I didn't write them down fast enough...
                                                    —Ruth Stone

There you were chatting on the radio as if
        you hadn't been dead for a week. I was driving
and weeping what I hadn't wept for a long time
        even for my own mother. How startling it is
to hear the dead speak after they're gone.
        When I got to work, I sat in the parking lot
watching the sky clear and the lake get
        smooth as glass. And what of those poems
out there in the ether, Ruth? If I were to stand
        at the lake's edge, tilt in just the right direction,
might the metal in my mouth pick them up?
        Might the skin? Might the hair on my head?
Might this heart? You hear about people getting
        radio stations in their teeth. Signals they
just can't explain. Yesterday, there were bear
        hunters in the field calling and whistling
for their dogs. The men were holding metal contraptions
        into the sky—looked like bicycle baskets
with aluminum foil patches hanging off them every
        which way. The men were tracking their dogs.
The dogs were out there somewhere in the woods, whooping.
        You could hear them rising up over one ridge,
disappearing down the next. They had their own business.
        Places they needed to get to.

Never Say You're Sorry

My black high-heeled Vince Camuto shoe is sitting
    in a snowbank somewhere downtown. Might have fallen
from the car when I dropped my son at The Daily Buzz,
    or my girlfriend at her job. It was time for class.
I was wearing my barn boots with the pink duct tape
    around the sole—manure, hay chaff, odd little bits
sticking out. I shuffled into school wearing those boots,
    passed out the papers I'd just graded. *Something stinks*,
one of the students said. We were studying death and taxes.
    We were seeking a female actor for the Ensemble. I had asked
the students to bring peanut butter or mac n' cheese.
    Next on the agenda was a critical look at Georgia O'Keefe.
My feet were too hot. The classroom desks were broken.
    Paint was peeling off the walls, and students had written on the desks,
Better Luck Next Time, and the usual *For a good Fuck, call...* etc. In the shop
    down the hall, teacher was teaching a welding course for women.
Oxy-fuel blazing. Oxy-fuel cutting. Business class was all about
    how to dun your debtors. I could hear the teacher running the students
through the drills. *You should set up a delinquency schedule
    and letters accordingly, and never, never say you're sorry,* she said.
I was thinking about my black high-heeled shoe in the snow-bank
    downtown somewhere. I was thinking about the cold air
inside it and the snowplows doing a final terrible scrape street by
    street. We were almost done with class; I was wearing paper shoes
on my feet at that point, compliments of the Chemistry teacher.
    The students looked up and saw a band of flashing lights
in the sky that were clearly not an airplane. They rushed
    to the windows but then the lights were gone. It just happened
to be the longest night of the year and there were celebrations to go to.
    One day perhaps I'll get the shoe back. A bit of salty snow
in the toe. And yes, I too saw the strange lights in the sky
    but I acted like nothing at all. I don't want to be the woman who
runs the UFO club. There's lots of things we people keep
    mum about. When I left class it was so quiet you could hear
my paper shoes rustling down the hallways. I've got the lone
    Vince Camuto on a special shelf in my closet.
If anyone out there finds the other one, please shoot me an email.

II

Pernath's Hat

The dreamer is at a social gathering. On leaving, he puts on a stranger's hat instead of his own.

...a stranger's hat imparts a strange personality... and as a result, the hero becomes involved in a strange experience...
—Carl Jung

There Being No Puppies

In a house with an aquarium and a giant goldfish
    glaring at me in a menacing manner, I was man-sitting

a friend's grown son who needed tending. I was not afraid
    of the fish threatening me through the glass.

What could it have done anyway? Just part of the territory,
    as was the man I was in charge of. I was sitting on the bed.

Things were going on in the house, and like the fish,
    the man got sinister. It happens sometimes. Next I knew,

he'd killed the dog. I told him, go down into the cellar and see the puppies.
    I said this in my sing-song voice. I was smiling big as you

can smile in these situations. It's something I've been working on.
    They say when you smile, you live longer. You get better jobs.

You make more money. I was smiling. My tone of voice
    was good. The man I was man-sitting went down the cellar stairs.

I locked the door behind him, but it was a worn-out button lock.
    I knew it wouldn't hold. I called the police. I called

friends. I called his mother who had once been my lover.
    We were together only a short time and she didn't remember

my name. I'm watching the door. Soon my man's
    going to burst from that cellar. There being no puppies whatsoever.

There Being a Dank Cellar

When she insisted on cranking up the music,
    twirling that hank of hair in her hands, the wet

flank of her face thanking us for the chance to
    rock and roll though the house stank of must,

there was water sloshing in the dank cellar
    as if the whole thing were some kind of tank

and whatever sank, sank. *Believe me,*
    no need to worry, she kept saying. *Whatever*

happens, happens! Each time she spanked
    her thigh, something clanked inside

me, that film between feeling okay
    and just plain panicky getting thinner

all the time. I was hoping it was some kind of
    prank finally, rank water shimmying

up to our door and the little boat yanking
    at its mooring as if there might be some dry

land to get to and a plank thick enough
    to step on when we got there.

The Requisite Bad Hair

The jig was up. We were in a room with many windows.
   A rag-tag boy army came down over the adjacent roof

and crashed into the room. Like in the movies.
   When the army boys came in, I was afraid they'd

get me, but I disguised myself as one of the locals just
   hanging out, poking through boxes in the basement.

Casual-like with no idea how I was going to get home.
   I picked a photo out of one of the boxes and was sure

it was a photo of my mother with a boy child I had
   never seen. Lately I'd been wondering about another

brother. If there had been one, and where he might
   have gone. The rag-tag boys gathered around me

while we all tried to figure it out. They were like
   Peter Pan's boys. Or Robin Hood's, but they'd been

up to no-good. One picked up the photo of my mother
   and started weeping. It turns out there's a weep in just about

anybody, but it wasn't his mother. Just the idea of it
   started him up. I pretended I didn't see anything.

Tried on a few shirts out of one of the boxes. Disguised
   myself as the lead singer in a grunge band none of us

had heard of. I had the clothes for it, some piercings
   in the right places. The requisite bad hair.

They were a good audience. Where they went to next
   I'm not sure, but that boy soldier took the photo with him

when he left. I went on with the grunge thing for a few years,
   but there comes a time in a person's life when enough is enough.

Some Random Trees

It was tax filing day and my roommate was feeling cheated.
    She kept walking in and out of the kitchen declaring

she wanted my cat though the cat had gone missing.
    I couldn't deal with it, so I went outside and took a ride

on my bike, closed my eyes at the wrong moment and
    ended up crashing into a garage. I was hanging around

hoping the cat would show up and afraid you know who
    might find him first. An old man was milling around

drinking cokes, answering phones. He opened the door—
    let in some stragglers no one should have let in.

Each one of them more pissed off than the next,
    but no cat. I was getting tired of it all, the old man

doddering around like my ex-husband for whom I do have sympathy
    no matter what. His heart was in the right place

but there was never anything behind it. You can have it
    like that, the heart just floating by itself in the chest

like a loose balloon in the sky. They get caught eventually,
    snagged on random trees, light poles, power lines.

Scraps of helium foil flashing. Though they are no good
    anymore they have a strange resiliency.

Lots of colors no matter what the weather, and always
    making me think of Maria's 5th birthday party,

the blindfolded children jumping up and down
    swinging sticks at a piñata none of them could break.

Where are those children now and whatever happened
to all those old men? I tell you the cat was like a jewel

to me. I went out and was calling and calling
for him. Sometimes I just don't know what to do anymore.

Some Brand-new Home-made Tattoos

There were hamburger patties left out on the counter,
    for how long, I didn't know, and didn't know

how long I'd be gone. The cat and dog were both
    begging for meat as they are wont to do. Cat jumped up

and grabbed a hunk. When my sport-coach father arrived
    at the house, I gave him a hug and told him I wasn't ready

to go. Yes, I had some odds and ends to clean up. He told me
    he'd be back in half an hour. Then I remembered he'd been

dead for ten years. I miss him now and then, but not his
    fierce temper. I think how in that small town we lived in

everyone knew what we were up to—we had to hide from
    our parents but got told on anyway. The phone would ring.

Someone would leak it. Whatever it was. There you are
    smoking a cigarette at the edge of the school yard,

or skipping choir practice, home-economics, math class.
    We always got caught. Should I be worried that my dead

father said he'd be back in half an hour? As in, *Your time
    is up. This is it. Get ready to go. You're done for.* He was always

a difficult one to hide from. When I go out now, I pull my hair
    over my face. Sometimes I paste on a moustache, yank my hat

down low. I've got some brand-new home-made tattoos.
    If you'd known me back then, you wouldn't know me now.

She Could Turn Up Anywhere

Yes, it was a small crime, but I was the perp.
  Myself and my girlfriend were being pursued

though the case was still under investigation.
  No one had anything on us yet. There was lots of

ducking down alleys. The usual crime show sort of thing.
  We were in a store and the detective, ever vigilant,

saw my girl, grabbed her, tried to arrest her.
  A shot was fired, and she ran. You need a girlfriend

like that always. One that can get away.
  I slipped out the door when a neatly coifed woman

pointed out where I'd gone. Somehow, I was running while
  watching her ratting me out. She was like those

teacher's pet girls I knew in first and second grade.
  After those grades most of us were no good.

It has to do with learning to read and write.
  How we give ourselves away. Some piece of paper

with evidence against me, something I had jotted down
  in an unguarded moment. I'd like to say

I had nothing to do with it. Finally, I ended up
  at my sister's house. She came into the bathroom

holding a sign with giant words printed on it:
  Get out. Run as fast as you can. Go! She put her finger

to her lips. The detective was right outside the door.
  He was yelling out the wrong name, but the crime was right.

The hunt was on. A body was involved. My girlfriend had gone
    underground. I don't know where she went. I do know

she could turn up anywhere. Once in a while she sends
    a coded message. I have no idea what it means.

Operation Children on Roof

I was part of the defending army, but I don't recall
    what war it was. Children were sitting on the roof

of a house at the edge of a cliff, seemingly unperturbed.
    Just watching. It was a long, tree-covered street.

Thick slabs of concrete tilted into a crater as big
    as a swimming pool. Cigarettes in their mouths,

Kalashnikovs strapped to their backs, five women
    guarded the crater. I had stupidly forgotten my shoes.

One of my friends had been shot by one of our cohorts.
    I took cover behind a tall blockade of sandbags,

sofas, sinks, freezers packed with concrete.
    Out of the ruins of a house a man walked toward us,

smiling. He was carrying a large white teddy bear.
    I nodded to my captain, however I'd forgotten a key

element of the maneuvers. I was carrying a long gun
    built like a giant weed whacker. Something you'd buzz

around the yard. I had some experience with those.
    But where was the safety on it? Some kind person

stepped in to show me the tiny blue slide that kept the gun
    from going off, and I was grateful. How good it is

that we can show gratitude in any kind of situation.
    Thank you, and *thank you*, I said, nodding. You'd think

I'd have been better equipped there being at least 130
    operations in the last 50 years. How pleasant we go on being

about it all. Operation Sand Bag. Operation
  Kids-on-the- roof- guarding-bombed-out

buildings. Operation Sand Storm. Whiplash.
  Infinite Reach.

Some Men in Plastic Cuffs

It was hard to find the courthouse tucked as it was down
    behind the orchard. Porches and pleasant porticoes

as if someone were living there. Not far from us,
    the lake shining and slapping on shore. Boats going past.

There were folding chairs set out for the defendants
    and their families. I'd been caught coming across

the bridge; my girlfriend caressing my hair
    and both of us laughing at the time. There were dings

in the car from grandfather back when I was a child
    and this was his car. Half-blind, me in the back seat,

Pop-pop driving, cracking into things. I scrambled
    into the front hoping to stomp on the brake, but my legs

were too short to be of use. It's like any other thing
    kids do in the company of grown-ups. That moment

when you see it's not going to be alright. Somehow
    we got home okay that day. I was recently mentioning

this to my grown daughter. How the Lincoln got the dents.
    That at the beginning of your life you don't know

what's going on, and then, like my grandfather
    towards the end, not a clue, but going the other way.

I'd been speeding on the bridge, yes. But not much.
    In court, I pleaded my innocence. This was after the men

in orange suits arrived at the building and lined up along
    the file cabinets. A young woman with a child in her arms

got up to greet her manacled boyfriend. He took his baby
    girl, held her in the circle of the cuffs. Some cooing

and nuzzling like nothing had gone wrong and was going to
   go on going wrong. Teenagers really. Still skinny. Complexions

blotchy. The chuckling sound the baby made when Dad
   shifted her in his arms. Little bubble of milk on her lips.

A Woman Trying to Save a Drowning Mouse

When I took the toilet and the vanity to the dump this morning,
   I saw a woman trying to rescue a bedraggled mouse

from the back of the garbage truck, packer blade in motion.
   She climbed in to get it. Tattoos on her arm. Plucky,

but stupid. The man in charge gave me a look
   as if to say, *clearly this one's from out of town.*

Something about the juice sluicing at the base
   of the truck's well, that stinking slurry and the obvious

condition of the mouse. It had already been through
   the sweep once; there was no hope for it. We like to think

there's hope for us all, yet when it's clearly over—
   we'll see it as such. No extraordinary means. No

climbing into the back of a garbage truck. Who wants
   to be dragged up out of that mess when we're already

done for? I went home and went to sleep and dreamed
   of an art museum. I was there with friends for something

called the Hamburger film, but the film was broken.
   I went out into the lobby. Long lines. Lots of traffic

on the street. Luckily there was a wailing wall in the lobby.
   You could put things into it. You could place your forehead

against it, let the cool stone comfort you. Like our mothers did
   when we had a fever. Sometimes you need something

touching the forehead. A cool hand. A large slab of stone.
   Sometimes you just need to rest your face.

Some Aggrieved Parties

My mother was getting sued though she'd been dead for a year.
    We were late arriving to court. The aggrieved parties

were already assembled. All the chairs taken. I went out,
    found some tiny folding ones like you'd have at the beach.

We were motley which is what we tended toward
    not having to get dressed up except for these sorts of things

every now and again. Some dress shoes. The same tweed
    jacket on my brother no matter the season. His one tie.

We had no idea what the charges against her were nor
    what anyone expected to get.

There was coffee to drink but it was muddy coffee.
    Lukewarm. Nothing our mother would have permitted.

She was good like that. The coffee hot. The milk not yet sour.
    We thought the judges were just warming up,

but it turns out court had been in session for hours.
    Robes unzipped; they'd been reading the material to themselves—

quietly turning pages; everyone in the courtroom watching.
    We had no idea what the procedure was. *It's a new world,*

I said to myself. Even the dead people guilty.
    There's that sound paper makes in a room full of people

sitting quietly doing nothing but breathing.
    I could hear a hint of music drifting down

the hill through the trees, or was that something still
    stuck in my head from a day I don't remember?

There Being a View of the Ocean

The condo was empty and near the ocean, so I moved in.
　　Turned out the rooms with the view were all at the other end

of the building, so I moved into the neighbor's place. Huge windows.
　　Books, tables. Better furniture than mine, and the ocean

banging and singing and hissing right outside the window. The super
　　came to talk to me and kept calling me Mr. Pendragle. I didn't care.

It was the name of the man whose home I'd moved into, whose bed I was
　　sleeping in, whose books I was enjoying, so I just nodded

and went along with it. It's a good thing to perfect. The nod.
　　A smile at the right moment. However, I realized I was about to be

discovered. Had left a bag of identifying pieces in my previous home.
　　I had to go get the bag. When I got to the old place,

I climbed the fire escape to get in as there was already someone else
　　living there, pretending to be me though I was no one,

and go on being so. I was thinking of Dylan Thomas having left
　　Under Milkwood in a bar. I was thinking

of the person who found that manuscript, and decided to be
　　Dylan Thomas, but was outed at a reading. The man wept

copiously. What else to do when you get outed? What to do
　　with that big bag of stuff? Did everybody already know

that Thomas had died of a heart attack in a different bar?
　　They took the body, but left the work behind. Lucky bartender

found it. Put on the tweed jacket. Poured himself a drink.
　　Had a few good nights on the poetry scene. It's all any of us hope for.

There Being the Thinnest Meow

I had forgotten the cat. She was a quiet cat but prone to
    disappearing into the furniture. Up into the ceiling.

An uncanny set of suction cup-like claws on her feet.
    I was missing her after I had forgotten her,

but I could not remember where I had last seen her.
    I'd been in the bank getting cash and remember

hearing something meowing. But maybe that was just
    my broken shoe. Or the woman next to me with a tic.

I took a cab home and the cabbie had a giant cat next to him
    on the passenger seat. I commented on that.

He said, *No ma'am this isn't a cat. It's my brother.*
    Four feet tall, fur all over the back of his head,

two furry ears pointing upward. I could even smell male
    cat habits wafting back to me. The cabby stroked

the brother's head and I clearly heard him purring.
    But it didn't help me find my own cat.

Or figure out where I had left it. *Kitty. Kitty. Kitty*,
    I keep calling. I rub myself on door jams around

town so kitty cat can smell that I am there. How can you say
    you've forgotten something when clearly you just plain

lost it? How can you complain that you lost it
    when you picked that cat out in the first place?

A cat the color of air. Eyes
    like smog. The thinnest most trickily meow.

Some Spilled Wine

My stepson wakes me to tell me
    he wants to go home. I sit up, spill a glass

of red wine on the mattress.
    Then the dog pees on the floor.

I'm going to have to compensate the landlord
    if I can't clean up the stains.

I get up, go to the corner store to buy
    stain remover, but the store

is closed. There's some men on the street
    I need to evade. One follows me

up the stairs—the daft, but likeable,
    very short and very odd man.

I've known him for a long time.
    I try not to hurt his feelings,

but I need him to leave. I tell him
    to go. *OK*, he says.

I get back into bed, turn out the lights.
    Later I realize he's still milling

around the apartment. I throw
    a pillow at him. I shout.

I want to complain to the landlord,
    but I know he's going to hold it against me.

The company I keep. The stairs I climbed.
    These stories I tell.

Some Details & Procedures

I was calling for the cat. I was walking down a road.
    My mother was in a hospital. I am missing many details.

I have the time sequence mixed up. It's what we do
    nowadays. I broke into the apartment to get something

my mother needed. Where the keys were none of us could say.
    I left a light on. I leave lights on. I left the radio on for the dog

that was living there. So he wouldn't look at me lonesome
    when I walked out that door. It was a sketchy poor dark street.

When I got back to the car everyone was waiting.
    My kids. My grandkids. We returned to the hospital. Big ward

with lots of beds and everybody sleeping. My mother
    was taking her last breaths so I took her hand and whispered

to her. She'd never been much of a hand-holder. *Not a hugger*,
    she used to say. I noticed how soft her hand was. There was a spot

of paint on her right palm. She'd been down to arts and crafts
    the day before. That same night I dreamed there was a giant

steep hill and I had to sit on top of the coffin as part of the burial.
    Apparently, it's how you bury the dead. You ride the box

to the bottom of a hill. Like riding a sled. It was a strange
    and terrifying burial. There was a fox yipping in a snowy

field. That human sound they make. I went looking
    for the painting she'd done the day before she died,

but it was already gone. Boxes packed. Bed stripped. How quick
    they are with the dead. How done.

III

It Was Out There the Whole Time

You made a monster and all you can think of is how sorry you are.
—*Circe*, Madeline Miller

When we brought the anaconda

home from the pet store things seemed to be okay. My sister insisted on carrying it around with her though she could barely walk the snake was so heavy. We were accustomed to that sort of extra load. Something a bit cool around the neck and the shoulders bowing down. I told her to put it back in the cage because we hadn't named it yet and didn't really know if it was a him or a her. She put a sock on the snake's tail that night because she was certain it would get too cold in our house, the heat hardly working and our father gone missing. The next morning the snake too was gone. There was no food in the house either and clearly the snake had rummaged through the cupboards. Had opened the fridge and drunk the milk. We saw beads of milk, and a ribbon of crumbs on the floor. Something we got used to hearing rustle around in the walls of the house all night long. It was like there was some extra muscle in our lives. One night my sister was giggling in her sleep and the snake was there around her middle pretending to tickle her. This is something that happens to girls. The thing wraps around you. You giggle. You forget.

To be honest, we were warned

about the bats. Thick belts of them flying from the houses and down under the bridges. The sound they made. The little beep-beep as they flew. How they would gather in the hair of children. Lift some of them up into the sky and take them with them. This was the common story when someone asked where so and so had gone. We were accustomed to it. Careful to put brick-like shoes on our children, we tied them into their carriages. Strapped them tight to the swings. *Push me higher,* they would shout. *Higher. Again. Again.* They didn't believe they'd ever get taken by the bats. And when they rode their bikes, which they insisted they be free to do, we made sure they had slick metal helmets covering their heads so the bats could get no purchase. It was not a good time for the children as you can well imagine. Nowadays, we have fewer of them. The bats. The children. Sometimes you see one of their faces on a poster around town, but mostly it's the dogs that go missing because dogs forget to check the sky above them. They get sloppy just trotting along sniffing out bits of shoe and hair and what not as they go, delighted there's a scent to follow. Something specific.

And when they gather

in the trees and make noise you know some other creature has downed something good to eat; the murder of crows trying to mob the killers off the killed. They rock back and forth at the tops of the trees. Barking orders. *Get out. Get out. That's mine. That could be mine.* I'd be a crow if my wings would work. How black my black would be. How shiny in the sun. Even the eagles would rise off the fields when I came round with my crew. I'd be a crow with a crew. I'd have the necessary muscle to move you down the road. If there was some gloss to my feathers. If I had a voice that could move you off that carcass you're on. Yesterday, in the woods behind my house, I woke to an owl clutching another owl in its talons, and the crows rocking the trees above them. The carcass too big for the owl to move, it pecked at it in the crotch of the tree. It tried to move it, then flopped with the dead to the ground. How the crows moved in closer. One thing to see the crows going for the carcass, another to see the owl trying to eat its own.

It was the summer there were herds

of tiny red deer on every corner, each lawn, under all the trees. Driving you had to sort of bump your way through them. They pressed up against our houses. Stared into living rooms, watched TV from the yard, joined the family at the picnic table, on the deck, at the lake. There was the sound of their breathing everywhere; they fogged up all the windows with their breath, left wet nose prints on babies in their carriages. We had to hire someone to move them back to the wilderness. He knocked on all our doors and asked each of us if *Jesus was our personal savior. Sure!* we all said. *No problem.* Jews, Muslims, Buddhists, Christians—all of us apparently had found Jesus. He said he'd take care of the problem. I miss them terribly though. Here I am staring at the edge of the woods. Waiting for them to step out and start grazing in the field. How suspicious they are now of all of us. Two-legged. Out of mind.

We were out in the park

     when the dirigible materialized above us. Slow but stealthy. The sun had been shining and the birds flying, but suddenly it all came to a halt. I know you don't believe this is possible, but I was there. The vessel was huge and most of us had never seen one up that close. Usually they were just way up above a football game with something quite harmless written on the side. This was different. Eggs started dropping out of the bottom of the dirigible. Gigantic Easter eggs. And yes, they were decorative, but it hurt when they hit. We took cover under the trees. We cried. We shook our hands at the blimp, but not much we could do to make it move. Music started tinkling out of it, like the music you hear on the Good Humor truck. The same riff over and over, and in your worst moments you think of the man who hid behind the truck with his zipper open and his stuff hanging out. So, you never told anyone about that. Neither did your daughter. Nor the daughter after her. So, no one ever told. Here's the truck. Here's the little tune. *Pop goes the Weasel. Around and around the Mulberry bush.*

Frogs were everywhere that night

If it rained frogs, I would say you had a point. —Bill Maher

as in a plague of. So many it was dangerous to drive. My heart sickens when I say this. How slippery the roads were. Finally, we stopped and just started walking, carefully stepping around them. They landed on our shoes, on our heads. We were coming home from town and arrived at the house covered in them. Tiny frogs singing in our hair, on our faces. My mother made me wash off outside with the hose, and the frogs reluctantly jumped down, went searching for the nearest tree as they were for the most part tree frogs. All night the trees bowed and sang. The air filled with that collective voice, and we knew we'd found something good to post on You Tube. Make some money. In truth, we had no idea if we'd make it through the next few years. I still have those videos. Myself standing in the moonlight, multi-colored frogs covering my body. If you could only hear the sound I made when I wriggled my skin, waved my hands above my head. I tell you, it was magical. I was a walking musical instrument. A bell choir. Some ancient DNA getting activated within me. Who cares I smelled like a swamp for a long time after?

When the archeologists

dug up the Giant Ape from our backyard I was not surprised. Certainly, something huge had been lurking there. Something with outsized teeth and long hair. Not your ex-husband, not mine, and not a lost dog. Something that could toss you over its back and step on you and there you'd be. I knew it was out there the whole time. It had to do with the ringing in my ears. And, of course with my bank account, and many of the bad decisions I've made along the way. I can hear them stirring—our original ancestors, the apes, pulling themselves hand over hand through the dirt. Would I like to see any of them right now? Yes, I would, but not in the way you might think. I keep pictures of them on the fridge. But still I'm not sure they'd be so glad to find me here at the table. Shivering in the cold. Pretty much hairless, and not so good in the trees. When they show up, they're going to want to know what I've been doing all this time. Why the table? Why the chair? Why that baffled look on my face?

They had her convinced

    they'd found her in a bees' nest, brushed her off. Kept her. Third brother told her getting born in that nest put her closer to a backwards god. Fourth brother said it put her closer to a hole in the earth she was always careful to avoid. The other brothers didn't mind either story. Every time they went past some buzzing spot, they pretended they had to grab her to make sure she didn't go back to her real mother. Years later, when third brother who hadn't talked to them for 20 years wrote to say if they were reading this letter it meant that he had died, she felt her skin change a bit. Heard that sound coming from her throat. Back in the day when she'd believed she wasn't really their sister but had just been found in a hive at the side of the road, she would walk into the part of the field where the bees nested. She let them crawl about on her hair, tried to teach them to speak. Did some sign language with them. She'd come walking out of the fields with that look on her face like she'd seen god. Bees in her hair. Some hornets riding her fingers. A tongue full of wings. Her hair gone golden with their bee bodies. Hornets. Honeybees. Some stingers. It did her good. The brothers a bit awe stricken and terrified. Her body making that sound. The boys all running to ground.

The pig strapped to the roof

of the bus squealed all the way one town to the next, but the iguana in the luggage rack made no noise. Now and again its owner took it down and showed it to people. I was not then acquainted with the idea that one might eat a lizard but apparently iguana is a delicacy. I would like to be back there now on that bus. I would like to be back in god knows how many places though liking and being are not the same thing. Even there on the Boston Common with the police on horses charging at us 1968. We were chanting, *The whole world is watching,* and apparently they were. This was back when there were just one or two TV shows and everything else was fuzz. One group of children scattering down one road at a time. One city. One beach-head-bunker- holding cell. What we do next is anyone's guess.

When the school of jellyfish

appeared around my boat this morning, flat white gelatinous plates pulsing bow to stern as if they might be floatation devices, I thought of the passengers on the Lusitania who'd fastened their life jackets on upside down. Funny for a second if it's not your story. Some were found days later feet up into the sky. Undignified. So much does that to us. You're in a panic. There's a hole in the boat and the stern cranking itself skyward, everybody tilting into the sea. The instructions are hard to read in those moments. Some had seen that luminescent wake coming directly at them but didn't know what it was. Who would think such a ship could sink so quickly? The sky blue, the sea flat. Land so close a person might think she could swim to it.

It seemed plausible

just like everything else did back then. The giant ape climbing the Empire State Building. The blonde in his hand screaming. Wriggling. The plan seemed straight on. I was a girl and I was blonde and there was that to look forward to. Getting grabbed around the waist and carried to the top of the building which led to the screaming my friend and I did in the haymow above my father's cows. *Just practicing,* we said after kissing and touching each other's breasts and then the screaming. I was never impressed by my own scream. It seemed to fall short. Not as good as Sandra's. Down in the barn below, the cows never stirred. Nobody could hear us up there in the mow. All those bales stacked around us. Field after field of tall grasses and small birds and whatever got caught in the baler stacked neatly to the ceiling. If you put bales away damp, they'll heat up, burst into flame. No matches. No smokes. If you put your hand in there, you can feel the heat. We were careful about it. But maybe that was just a myth. Barns catching themselves on fire. Point of origin unknown.

We'd taken to being clever,

or is that merely mischievous? We knew the difference between sensible and insane. The circus animals in the neighbor's backyard should never have been there in the first place. We were at the age of clarity about so many things. Lions, tigers, one baby elephant, two bears. Why not take the lion cub home and let all the rest of them out? Everything looked tame and quite manageable. Mostly toothless, though when we opened the gate to the tiger's cage, we realized we'd done something we might not should have done. There're lessons to learn, we knew that, and now and again you might have some time left in your life to apply those. No matter, we took the cub home. Grateful to us and glad for the attention, she stood over the bed until we went to sleep. She hid under the covers during the day. Our mother had no idea we had her though the room was starting to take on a peculiarly feral odor. Certain it was just the change of life happening to us, some blood, some breasts and hair—no one was that concerned. Everything gets a bit feral when it comes of age. When either parent walked into my room, they did so cautiously. Like they were entering foreign territory. Neighborhood chickens were beginning to disappear. And small dogs. When we pulled the covers up to our chins, there was that purring sound in the room almost like a car idling somewhere in the neighborhood, but no telling where. Which neighbor.

You can hear them moving

in the closets but you're not sure if that's the sound of your breathing or something else alive in the house. There's that hole in the blanket you can't explain. Moth, or mouse. Whatever it is in the house that's eating things surreptitiously. It's the surreptitious that gets to us. Small bites out of things you loved. It's the life of a house. Something in the wall. Something chewing. In summer the flocks of them around the lights. Notorious for their ability to impersonate other creatures—nothing a bird would want to eat. Which is how so much arrives and departs. Something pretty dressed up like something frightening or vice versa: nothing you'd want to pop in your mouth. It looks delectable but tastes like dust. How easy it is to get your signs mixed up, mistaking love for trouble and trouble for love. The heat that trouble makes. Drawn to it some might say. That candle flame. That light on the porch. The dust of wings. That tooth.

He was outside digging

for night-crawlers when I got home. The flashlight, little bucket, tiny whistle he used to entice them out of the ground. He was a magician really the way they'd come out of their holes and look around. Blinded suddenly by the light, they'd stop wriggling, let him pick them up between his index and thumb. They're never warm to the touch, and he would want to warm them a bit like somehow it would make it all better. What he was about to do. The hook he'd pass through the night-crawler's tubular rubber. Only it wasn't rubber and the hook was the hook. The stream, the stream. And the fish swimming with its mouth open, the fish. I wasn't a fan of that. Hauling the fish out of the stream. The stream was in the fish and the fish was cold to touch. The eye like the eye of the sky. Like the eye of anything that might look at you if it could. How we need them though. What we eat. What we haul out of the stream. What we hook through the lip.

So if you see the owl

and it turns its head and stares back at you with its satellite dish of a face, and the next day your dog gets quilled and a tiny piece of one of your teeth chips off, does an owl in the tree at dusk mean you better watch yourself? If you forgot to watch yourself doesn't that mean that you've moved to a better spiritual plane? If you believe in that. If you don't believe in God and you say to someone, *I'm sending you my prayers*, are you lying to that person? If you are lying to that person is the owl going to say its prayers and the dog get quilled? If the owl quills your porcupine will something horrible happen to your dog? And yes, we are full of questions. One after the other. We are a wind that didn't know how it got where it is. But the time is short. The day almost over. There's the owl again. Its quills gleaming in the moonlight. Here's the dog scratching at the door. There's the print his nose makes on the glass.

I didn't know her raising rats

in the backyard shed would be a problem, the chirping sounds they made when they heard her coming through the grass. How they liked to be tickled. How she liked teaching them about the psychological benefits of laughter. From time to time, you could hear her laughing above the chirp. I thought maybe she was telling herself jokes. Thought maybe she had somebody out there with her. Some kind of affair I didn't know about. Otherwise, no problem, except when the neighbor's pet python heard what was going on and came slippery slidey out of his cage. Who could blame him for not being able to resist that laughter? If you're not the one laughing it can make you feel a bit lonesome. Maybe he was lonesome. Hearing it from one yard over. All that tickling.

Imagine sliding out into the yard in that moonlight so sad as he was and hearing all that giggling. Maybe he just wanted to see what was going on in the shed. Maybe he just wanted to touch some of that happiness. Perhaps he needed to hold it in his mouth. How we do do that if it's something really good. You want to touch it with your tongue. Taste it before swallowing. Feel it in your own belly. The snake thought it would be so good having all that inside himself. That he could swallow it and love it all at once. He imagined himself laying out in some sunny spot somewhere, out of his mouth some giggling. Some belly laughs. His own little spot of happy.

Befuddled bees on the bike path

with honey I would have satisfied you

in three pizza-platter size clusters. No sweet on the asphalt. Nothing to eat. Nowhere to nest. Some misfired cue. Bicycle riders riding quick as we can through them there being no way around. River on one side. Marina channel on the other. Hold your breath. Don't breathe in the bees. Sun-beaten wind buzzing. Dazzle of bees on the pavement. Giant humming plates of themselves. Clutching his forehead, a boy pedals toward me screaming he's been stung. He doesn't stop. No one stops here. A man says to deal with reality you must first recognize it as such. Buzzing heart, lungs, the skein of sting. Errant Queen at the center of each plate. I pedal quick as I can, beach tar stuck to my feet—those black globs of oil I mistook for sea rocks. I had no idea I was stepping in it. Cellophane wings. Yellow stingers singing. Offered up like a meal you could eat if only you could eat bees. If only you could wear them on your face. Your legs. Your tar-spotted feet buzzing.

It seemed like a good omen, a robin

nesting on the ladder hanging along the back side of the house I was just moving into. Everything of course, a sign. The cemetery across the street. Its tallest tombstone. The apple trees. The flowers I couldn't name in the garden. Five robin eggs in the nest. Such blue. Then the naked, bald hatchlings. Yellow-rimmed mouths open but the eyes still shut. Fat-bellied like clam bellies. Two days later, the nest torn open on the ground. Baby robins scattered. Killed but not eaten. Some bird cleaning its territory of other types. Balloon bellies swollen; heads pecked off; flies starting in on the corpses. Burying them, I eyed the surrounding trees—various birds singing and warbling. And, of course there's that talk of evolution. That we came from the fishes, started walking on land. Lost the excessive hair on our backs, learned to use tools. That supposedly unlike the wolves and lions, we don't kill other people's young for territory. That the organism has something grander on its mind than simply making sure its genetic material continues, tribe by tribe. How we humans love the bird song all around us. I like to think the singing is simply singing, and never just trumpeting over territory: *Here I am. This is mine. This is mine. Get the fuck out. Who cooks for you?* You see the birdwatchers gathered in odd spots. Everyone staring up at something in the bushes. Binoculars raised. Mouths open. Careful not to make any quick moves.

My mother kept sparrows

in the back of the drying yard out of sight along with underwear, t-shirts, jeans, blouses, little birds in her hands. I'd spy on her through a hole in the fence. Hold my breath so I wouldn't spook her. It was like she had another family altogether. Mother cooing to them. Mother stroking their heads singing in that thready voice she had. She was trying at one point to make them do tricks. Like they were little dogs in the circus or something. Fly through the neck holes of t-shirts. Hang upside down on the line. Carry the clothes pins back to the clothes pin bag. This was her secret. The song she sang in the drying yard. The flicker of sparrow wings in and out of her fingers.

Always someone or other in the family keeping something—baby squirrels in a bedroom drawer, fawn in the basement. The squirrels grew up and took off. As did the fawn. As did the sparrows my mother kept. As did the drying yard and the laundry we hung there. As did my mother and the t-shirts we wore. You might think it sad that the drying yard was my mother's only private place. I remember how she smelled when she came back into the house. A certain glow on her face. She'd hum as she folded the clothes. At school, we'd find tiny feathers in our shirts and socks. Odd bits of something in every sandwich.

Roaming in multitudinous herds,

       seemingly un-perturbed—their competent dark bodies strutting across roads, populating fields. You'd think you could catch them, but they're wily. I put out a net beside the goldfish pond. I waited patiently until a large hen walked right into it. She was upset, but finally acquiesced and allowed me to disentangle her after I'd given her some apple cake with raisins in it. She was reluctant at first to move in with me but that had been my plan all along. I had wanted her for a meal, but I grew fond of her. Following me around the house like a dog. Pecking at the ladybugs that slipped in through cracks when the day heated up to 60. After a while though, I felt like I was being watched. Every time I got up from bed, she jumped up and went with me. Sitting on the couch watching TV. There she'd be. Liking, and not liking the shows. Clicking her nails on the floor. All that scratching, chirring, and clucking. I was annoyed one day when I found her poking through the fridge, approving. disapproving. What she did when I got dressed to go out. A look in her eyes that told me I shouldn't go anywhere dressed like that.

Now I blame my agoraphobia on her. My reluctance to drive at night. My all-around lassitude. I blame her for the fact I've made some bad decisions. Even the ones before she came along. And current events even. Push came to shove when she started making my friends uncomfortable. She'd sit up in a chair when somebody came over, stare at them while jerking her head back and forth. Finally I took to putting her in the pantry when anyone showed up. But she just putted and kicked. My new love interest didn't even know about her but of course suspected something. Might have been the look in my eyes when I said, *Oh it's just some branches tapping and clicking at the window.* Girlfriend knew it wasn't the weather. One day, *I love you, I love you*, and the next, girlfriend was gone. Not to worry. My heart is spotless now. My living room completely free of bugs.

I know it was not nice of me

Genghis Khan reportedly decided not to conquer India after meeting a unicorn, which bowed down to him; he viewed it as a sign from his dead father and turned his army back.

but when they brought the twins to stay with us, I told them freaky stories so they might go home and I'd be the only daughter again, flawed as I was. They were good girls with blonde hair and why they'd come to stay with us I don't know but I didn't want them. We had enough children already elbow to elbow. Like many other gullible girls at that time they were obsessed with fairy tale animals, unicorns and the like. I told them I was the only one could ride the unicorn they'd seen running one night across the field. In truth it was my white horse cleaned up with a stick on her head. I loved thinking of Sheila and Sharon staring out the window as I rode by. I was a magical girl. A girl with something up her sleeve and the competent white haunches of my horse pumping beneath me. I told them my mare had many foals hidden in the grove of pines behind the swamp. I said if you go out there you can get your own baby unicorn. I wanted them gone. But lately I've been thinking of them. About mean children. What we get born with and what goes missing. I watched as the two of them went quietly into the woods to see if they could get one for themselves. The sight of Sheila and Sharon's golden curls bobbing at the back of their heads as they walked into the forest stays with me. I have no idea what happened next.

Having watched *The Red Pony*,

we children knew vultures meant something you loved was done for. There the dark birds circled, and there you'd find your heartbreak. Something formal like that. Then the scrum of birds roiling on a carcass, pulling out entrails—their dark wings thudding. Lately I have been using euphemisms. When my mother died, I called my brother and said, *She's gone.* As if she'd simply put her oxygen down and wandered from the home. When we buried her, we buried her in an urn. Said some home-made prayers. Sang a couple of songs. You can dig the hole yourself. It was the digging broke my brother down—the scritch of metal into stony dirt. Yesterday, at my neighborhood cemetery, a glossy black hearse shouldered the top of the hill. A small circle of people gathered and the dirt piled up with that green rug on top of it Sometimes you don't want the dirt to look like dirt. You want the long black car there. Someone in a suit. Doors that open and shut. A vehicle you could climb inside. Tinted windows and fat cushions you could slump down into. Your life not your life in that moment but something with formal dimensions. You want to put the broken part of you into something plumb. Immaculately polished. Sometimes you just want someone there who knows the words.

You do not want them

in your fields. The holes they make. Places your animals could step into and break a leg. Mounds that could tip a tractor over if the kids were driving and weren't so smooth letting out the clutch. And yes, this is a farm story which is what those of us who grew up on farms have always secretly known is the only story. The death. The sex. The birth. The father beating on the cow. The pig getting its throat slit. How you watched whatever happened to be happening and you didn't flinch. Two brand new hooves poking out the backend of the cow. Then the wet muzzle. The face. Then the whole calf body slipping out, thumping onto the ground. There you have it. The wet. The mess of it. The stories we told each other. The guy who dropped a pitchfork out of the hay loft on a man who showed up at the farm from time to time. The hunch of his back. How we eyeballed him. The place the fork landed. And the calf just born in the barnyard. Getting up on its spindly legs. Out of the slops. My dog rushing out to eat the placenta. The afterbirth. All that licking and chewing. My dog. How sharp her eyesight. She'd spot a woodchuck from the top of the pasture and off she'd go. How many times I watched her sprint through the field, grab a woodchuck by the neck and shake it dead. She'd bring it back. Roll in it. Eat it. She was the dog that went everywhere with me. She had murder in her; it's true I liked that. I was a girl in need of some murder. The sharpshooter that was my dog. I was a girl in need of something running fast-fuck down the field and shaking it by the neck.

We've been standing around

Xenoceratop: Latin for alien horned-face from foremost

for the past few days wondering how the fuck it had happened. Things had been going along fairly well. Everybody hopeful. Until the you-know-what appeared in Jack's backyard. Something had gone wrong in the university lab up the street. Cells had been cloned but the cells mixed with the cells of the neighborhood's missing python or something else we hadn't known about. Hard to tell though. When Jack started shooting at it, we knew we had a problem. The creature had been calm, but now it seemed to be in must. Hungry for something but it wasn't sure what. It's a familiar hunger. Feathers on its hind legs, plated skin thick as armor and the five purple-tipped horns on its back. Those who'd heard about the cloning experiment felt somewhat responsible for what happened though Jack had been a problem for a long time already. Target practice in his yard all hours of the day and night—AK- 47's, Glocks, Tannerite. Imagine Jack's delight to see the creature looking in the window at him. Scraping its horns along the side of the house, the crackling, hissing sound it made somewhere down in its throat. If you could have called what it had there, a throat. No one wants to talk about what happened to Jack. What we found when the beast left the premises. Where it might turn up next.

When my mother and I

went shopping for clothes I may as well have had yellow jackets under my skin. The stinging kind. The kind that make you fat and queer. Something buzzing in me that didn't work for her. Something in her that didn't like what she saw. It's like when you're picnicking in a warm fall day and get swarmed by yellow jackets. There they'd be on the apples, on the rims of the glasses, in the cakes, and on your mouth. Everything you picked up to put in your mouth had something buzzing on top of it. We were like that. She and I. *Watch what you eat,* she'd say. You have to admire them. Their tenacity. *Meat bees*, they're erroneously called as they do not eat meat. You might hope you could train them seeing as they form columns and organized nests, but try as I might, they flew off in multiple directions. When I think of her now, I feel some movement beneath my skin, mottled as it is at this point. Perhaps it's that ringing in my ears—the yellow jackets in their best yellows. Racing colors as they say at the track though we're not at the track. I do miss her nonetheless no matter what I tell you next.

It is true what they say

about zebras. Like your squirrels, your raccoons, the fox my father had as little boy. Wild. And they never stop being wild. You can't domesticate them. Some of all of this should never be domesticated. Something should never be ridden. Such a strong back the zebra has but don't put a saddle on it. There in the picture the 210 lb man on the zebra's back, his cowboy boots touching the ground. Believe me, this is a rare occasion—a rare zebra. I was a rare child. We had a rare herd— zebras mixed in with the Holsteins and the Belted Galloways. It's the black and white of it all. The pattern of paradox. Opposite forces right there on the skin. The Yin, the Yang. The girl who wanted to be a boy. The hate love thing. The queer as it comes thing. You can stand in the shadow and look like the shadow. Can stand in the light and look like the light with cracks in it. The dark stripes that light has sometimes. The in and out of it. I was the black and white girl. I rode the zebras and no one could tell where the zebra ended and the girl began. My hair the color of sky. My eyes the green grass. It was a trick I learned. How to blend in with what needed blending in with. It's a queer thing really. How to look like you're loving the event but secretly you want to go into the back field, catch fireflies on your eyelids. You want to get up on that zebra and ride away but they're a stubborn lot. They don't come when they're called. Some say they're jerks. Some say what's she doing now? Out there in the field whistling, whistling the crickets up around my ankles and that black and white shape moving towards me.

IV

How We Came Up Out of the Swamp

Darwin's theory of evolution is the widely held notion that all life is related and has descended from a common ancestor: the birds and the bananas, the fishes and the flowers—all related.

Nothing But Blue Skies

Here comes the song my mother used to sing when she was packing up
  to die *Blue Skies, Nothing but Blue Skies* here come the blue skies
here comes my mother with her blind eyes peering up to the sky my
  mother singing while I drove and here comes me driving that road here
come the spaces between places which some like to think are short and not
  inked in with something you can barely see but goes on and on as you
drive your long dead mother singing in the seat next to you
  Que sera, sera she sang when she was just hanging out with her girls
until I told her she had to stop with that song here comes that song in my
  mouth here it comes those vowels scratching from my throat my voice
not much better than hers that wispy sound she made sometimes calling
  to say she was lonely where she was here it comes *Just a little bluebird*
in the wilderness waiting for the end to come she sang in the hospital
  until I told her *Just a little bluebird waiting to be fed* was the true line
but it was her song and here they come those ditties she sang in her last
  two years wishing all the time there was some man around and not just these
weepy daughters shushing her here comes the word *dumb* which I uttered
  yesterday about myself turning down the wrong hall having locked keys
in my office which is what she used to say about herself about when she
  found herself with that little bit of eyesight left and those Blue skies nothing
but blue skies tilting her head she'd say *Oh look at those jet trails*
  but who knows how she could see jet trails blind as she was here comes
the road she was driving when we didn't know she couldn't see but later
  told us *Oh I just find the white line and stick by it* here it comes that white
line down the side of the road and here comes my mother holding to it.

What Month Is This? What Year?

Finally you end up being naked places you never imagined yourself naked
in plain sight of people before whom you were always impeccably clothed,
as in your sons and daughters learning now to touch your skin.
If your skin was your own business at this point, something private.

In plain sight of people before whom you were always impeccably clothed,
we touch your hair, smooth down the spot you missed with the brush.
Your skin no longer your own business at this point. Nothing private.
My brother and I exchange looks above your head. We nod at the doctor.

We touch your hair, smooth down the spot you missed with the brush.
You pick at a red mark on your forehead; I put your hands in your lap.
My brother and I exchange looks above your head. We nod at the doctor.
He taps your back. Asks you questions. What month is this? What year?

He doesn't scold about the red marks. You keep your hands in your lap.
Trained as you were as a child to sit up straight. Polite. Obedient.
Dr. listens to your heart. He wants to know what month this is, mother,
what year. You answer carefully as if there were some comfort in it.

Trained as you were as a child to sit up straight. Obedient.
Your sons and your daughters learning now to touch your skin.
You answer each question thoroughly as if there were some comfort in it,
sitting up naked in places you never imagined yourself naked.

GPS

It's shorter than you thought it would be or
   maybe longer. And beauty itself unabashed running
north to south, east to west across the lake. What else

is there? Dog nudges the hand that feeds him.
   The dead get spotted all day long in various places.
A GPS almost. Little dots on a map

and the grown children standing around a bit dumbfounded.

The Loving Family Van
—via Amazon.com

i thought it would be nice to have a vehicle to transport the family
    around town however the quality and design is somewhat lacking

the back doors fall off all the time both my husband and daughter
keep knocking the doors off they are not well made only the adults fit in

the front we have two families and the grandmother it is difficult
to get them all in the car at once we can fit three small people in the back

seat but dad's feet and shoulders make it difficult to get him in and out
of the car the limbs are NOT articulated the mothers keep sliding

under the dash our youngster has removed arms heads legs who cares
if the mom doll isn't pretty the child certainly won't the van comes

with a dog and a bag of groceries though I am not sure why the dog
was included but it's ok I worry that the doors will not go back on as with

most of the loving family items the design is poor but they are a lot of fun

Musac

We do not expect to be bludgeoned by laughter and/or by love
or other pleasantries, and neither do we expect music to be used on us.
If there were some kind of ordinance against it. What they do with it
in public places. As if to placate us, subdue us. Help us not hear
what the ones in charge of the place are chattering about. As if
to make us stand calmly in the elevator. In the customer service line.
As if to put something inside us. As if to make us dance.
As if the songs we used to sing to could be flattened like that.
As if to flatten out the years when we danced to that music.
The airwave goes into your ear. It is a physical thing. It's a thing.
You can measure it; you can talk about it in physics class.
I was in the airport after flying all night but it was still night
in the place I'd come from and it wasn't yet morning in the place
I'd landed. So I tried to sleep but they were singing at me.
Wind Beneath My Wings next to *See You in September*; something
you would know the words to if you realized you were listening,
and indeed you are, those notes having inserted themselves
into the lobe of the brain where some vague and not particularly
flattering memory lingers. I sat up in my chair with my feet
on the suitcase and my head against the wall. The arms
of the chair immovable. To keep us from lying down and sleeping.
To keep us from our worst impulses. I nodded off for a minute,
then the voice on the PA broke in warning us to take our pets
outside to do their business. As if that would keep the stray sparrows
from defecating on any of us. You see them flying
about the airport terminal as if it were the place they were supposed to be.
Like it was fortunate to be here. Picking up crumbs
from exhausted passengers. Drinking from water fountains.
Perched in places nobody could touch. As if we had a right to expect
some kind of uniform behavior, the same for our pets as for the wild
animals flying through the open doors in spite of security.
Unless the birds themselves are some kind of security.
Lifelike and all. Omnipresent. Able to dart in and out
of the most interesting places. I closed my eyes
listening to the latest version of smooth Beatles—
Love, love me do, then *Maybe I'm just like my mother, she's never
satisfied*, that loop of sound indefatigable. Eternal.
Sharps rounded off. Flats shaved. Smooth as water.

Like any other thing that could easily drown us.
You've got to know when to walk away, know when to run.
Go ahead sway to that tune, shake your hips in your chair.
You'll forget the name of the song but there you'll be
humming it when you least expect it. A bit off key,
the words in your head slightly screwy.

Walking the Ice

tracks of animals that went walking
   on the frozen river today

light enough to stand anywhere
   to walk one frozen block at a time

water banging along beneath
   ready to take whatever weighs

too much the river not a river
   you might be able to step across it one

chunk to another I hold my breath as
   the dog follows a scent into the center no

telling where there might be a gap
   covered by this dust of new snow

and I think of Barbara who rode ice floes
   on the Connecticut as a child leaping one

to another who leapt inside out who
   died of a brain tumor just down river

from Vernon who never paid taxes who
   rode under that wire who died at 33 who

made love to me in that cabin in Wendell
   no water no electricity no phone the weed

we smoked the Jameson the wood stove
   burning who vowed she would not

die in the hospital would take herself out
   into the woods and end it but she

held onto it this thing we cling to ragged
   as it gets rapturous today the sunlight on new snow

Ode to Smoke

On the plane with my mother, barely 17, I lit up, I struck a match, I lit the cigarette. It was when you could smoke in all the places you went. On buses, trains. We sat and smoked. Plumes of smoke lifting from our seats. We were all smokers. We shared, we took it in together, on planes and buses, smokers huddled in the back, the non-smokers coughing but okay with it, or not okay with it, but what could they do? We rode around with my father's unfiltered Chesterfields burning in the car then stole them from him, went out into the fields to smoke. When we couldn't find the smokes we smoked straws. We went into the cornfields and made corn-cob pipes and smoked them. We burned what we could and breathed in the smoke. You could see us huddled in the dark, way beyond the house, the red tips of whatever we were smoking bobbing up and down. We learned how to smoke backwards, how to hold the tip inside the mouth and smoke. Later we smoked joints, we blew smoke from one mouth into another. We filled each other with smoke. We became bold with smoke. We smoked in school bathrooms, someone watching in the hallway. When teacher came in, the room was filled with smoke, and the girls with their red lipstick and fishnet stockings, rings of smoke out our noses, but no one smoking. We smelled bad. Everybody did. It was something to share, intimate in its way. Teacher standing there in the doorway of a room of teenage girls with their fresh but pimpled faces and smelling of smoke. Our fingers were stained as if we had been painting with smoke, tattooed by smoke. You could lift your fingers to your nose, you could smoke the fingers. Assuage yourself. Comfort yourself a bit. If we didn't have money for them, we stole them. We stole them from mother's purse. We stole them from stores. We picked up good butts off the streets. The cars we drove in were filled up with it. There was nothing but the fog of smoke. Clouds you could see coming in and out of us. We had lit ends in our hands. We carried matches. We carried lighters. We were never without smoke. We sometimes rolled the ends of cigarettes we found in ashtrays. We bought loose tobacco and we rolled it up. We were smokers and we were not ashamed to be smoking. To be walking around with that lit thing. To throw them lit from the windows of cars. To watch the embers explode backwards on the highway. Now and then someone's habit burning little holes in their clothes. There were holes in everything. Little black burns on counter tops, on tables. On carpets. Bedspreads. We snuffed them out on the floors. It was everywhere around us. The teacher smoked. The doctor smoked. Mother smoked. And where do we linger now that we quit? That cigarette turned round backwards. The lit end inside us. Where did we go? Can you still smell it on us when we walk by? We would light up if we could. We need a smoke now. We need some grey fog billowing around us. We need some calming down. Some giant weed burning between our lips. The balconies are emptied of us. The back lots are cleared of our butts. Our cars smell like cars. Our hair is shiny. Nobody's standing outside the back door burning. There's nothing on fire.

The Good Dark

Brother hatching pigeon eggs in the cellar closet
can't wait to see how big the chick inside is.

Holds the egg to the light, shakes it. Then cracks it
open. No way to see until it's broken.

Yolk in his hand. Bits of feather. That stink.
Myself watching reality TV show in Tucson taco shop.

One man serving another man papers. I think of
that stink in brother's hand. Lots of fuck you and fuck off.

Two men shoving and shouting. Riveting.
Everything in plain sight. Someone's worse thing.

Men smacking each other around. Fist to face to
gut and back again. As if to kill each other.

Which is how we went at it as kids.
Slugging. Biting. Kicking. No

mincing and faltering. Nothing scared us. Just
our Father coming around the corner.

He's gone. Mother's gone. The siblings up next.
Bum heart. Errant cells. Whatever it is. Children

sent into the field to pick sweet corn because we were
the children and did what we were told, ripped

ears from stalks. Tore each one open.
Anything wormy got chucked. Wave after wave

of green leaves rustling on themselves. Nothing
anyone could take a picture of.

The good dark between rows. The ripping sound the sheathes
of green made getting peeled back from the fruit.

Kettle Pond

The experience of rock. Of rock after rock. Granite, feldspar, quartz
    covered in moss, fern, tucking up to the lake. Stepping through rocks.
Up. Down on rock. Avoiding holes between rocks. And the water
    shimmering through the tent of trees. Granite. The stability of it.
Rising up underfoot. Making its own light it seems. Rock. Hand
    by hand on rock. The cells of which do not rearrange themselves.
The molecules of which do not grow into something that could kill it.
    The earth with its sturdy floor. Its piles of duff. Its bits of broken
trees and fallen leaves. Distracted by voices, I looked up. Tripped
    on a rock, banged down flat on my chest. Hit the door of the earth
and it didn't open. I'd been thinking about permeability. About
    the plastic port being put in my sister's chest 2600 miles away,
the body being opened, that small cluster of cells threatening her life.
    And then I fell onto the earth. The breath knocked from me, as if
something in me needed to get hit too. Bruised wrist, arms aching,
    but nothing broken. Skin intact. Earth intact. I rested at the edge of
the pond. One massive boulder lifting from it like the hull of a white ship
    coming to shore. Monolithic. Light gleaming from inside the rock. On
top of it. Cupping it. The lip of the sky passing across the day.

The Fires in Pioneertown

I get all my comfort from nature, she said and there was nothing
anyone could tell her. I wanted to hold her, wanted her to hold

me but she was obdurate as in refusing to change one's course
of action, as in mulish. Pig-headed. In-flexible. When I see palm

fronds glittering in the sky, I am reminded how we loved each other—
the touch of her skin on mine, her hand entering my body but when

we broke, we broke hard like the neighbors across the valley
fleeing the fires. Un-able to save their animals, they left everything

behind. Nothing but cellar holes, chimneys, metal posts remained.
Three nights the fires burned, flames igniting the pines one by one.

Sometimes I remember this in my body, grateful as I am to it
for taking me this far, for how desire links one place to another.

The skin and tongue and hand of it. Every time I think of her,
I wish all of us well. What we break. What we can't fix.

Ode to Blundering

I want to think that the two downy woodpeckers
    pecking the lichen on the beloved but partly
ruined apple tree outside my window are helping the tree,
    as I like to think the snow banked up solid four feet tall
against the back door is somehow good
    for the house, all that weight leaning on it and the snow
expanding, contracting, helping it stand to in the wind,
    just as I like to think the mistakes I've made
have somehow given me extra points as in coupons
    and mileage and free gifts I could use later
when push comes to shove, and I
    especially like to think there should be an age limit
on our stupidity, our willingness to believe
    the voices whispering in our ears: *Love, love me do,*
you sweet something, etc., but even Lear was
    duped, and Hamlet Sr. fell fast asleep in the garden
with his ear pointing up to the sky, his jealous
    brother lurking behind the screen with that vial
of poison trembling in his hand. You want to shout
    at those old men, shake them by their white
heads like they were fat puppies. Smack them awake.
    All of us older and none the wiser—grey bearded
spindly- headed- spotted-palsied- hands held out
    in front of us, what else to do but get on with it—
blunder, then blunder some more. *Mi amor, mi*
    amor, she whispered, and there I went.

Loops, Spins and Hammerheads

Is this the gain of a new feature, or drastic selective
sweep, the pilot in the small red plane yesterday
doing flips above the lake, engine revving up, then the plane
looping backward to fly upside down half a minute?
It sounded like an accident about to happen but then
everything came round right-side up again, over and
over. Maybe that's where we're going—this last
afternoon before the clocks get turned back.
Before dark comes at 4:30 pm. Before we all just do
what we're told once again. Go around the house adjusting
clocks. Numbers flashing at us. The plane up
ending. That fuck-you to what we should be doing to
stay safe. To safe flying. That bit of joy up there in the sky,
everyone on board screaming and laughing. Hanging
for a minute by their belts upside down above the earth.
Making like a crash, but then not crashing. The next
logical step perhaps. Some sort of artful adaptation.

Embryos with Teeth

The rough-skinned newt produces high levels of toxin
to which the garter snake has developed equal levels of
resistance. The newt specially designed for slow travel
across ground and the garter snake prepping for a meal.
The co-evolution of the feeder and the fed-upon.
Which brings me to the dinosaurs. Bits of their DNA
still following us around. Their tracks printed
in the mud of this valley. Three-toed creatures
40 feet long. Heads the size of dorm fridges.
How is it they didn't just topple over at the slightest?
I imagine the air was thicker then. The molecules large enough
to prop them up. Something worked for them
and then suddenly nothing did. How frightening
some of the ones who came after them are. One
stealthy cell at a time. The body trying to outfit itself.
Invent a new currency. Scales. Gills. Chickens growing
embryos with teeth similar to those of crocodiles.
A new egg. Something sweet to eat. Some loose talk.

Déjà-vu, or How We Got Out of the Swamp

Maybe it's not déjà-vu. Maybe I've just been pretty busy
repeating myself. Dialogue exact. Trees in the right places.
Nothing spooky about it at all. Guys and gals kicking
their legs in the air. Audience singing along.
The whole score memorized years ago. We like thinking
it's the spirit world talking to us. Something Edgar Allan Poe
about it. And where did that teacher go who read us
those stories with such aplomb? We were 12, 13, ready for the world
being that strange, and all our actions coming back at us.
Missing Cat. Heart bricked up in a wall. People milling
about in the street. It's coming back to me now. The audience
restive. Someone out there in the dark with a tickle in her throat.

*

Lately I've been thinking about evolution. How we came up
out of the swamp. Crick in the throat, some part of us
trying to breathe but the breathing piece missing.
No gills. No fins. And the air impossible. Today,
the saleswoman on her I-Pad tapping inch-long
glossy nails against the screen. All of us waiting
for central office to explain some bizarre new charge
on the rental car. Something I wasn't going to pay.
All systems were down. There was a bargain somewhere,
but it was making me too nervous.

*

It was making me too nervous. I had to
get out of there, took myself directly to the beach.
Needed to stand in some sunshine, float
in the sparkling blue waves. The sun
had come out for the first time in days.
The president was flying into town, his updated helicopters
hovering over the beach. Like supplicants anywhere,
we were jumping up and down in the sand,
waving our phones in our hands, shouting,
trying to snap his face at the window but which window
was he sitting at? Which chopper? One might wonder
what to make of all this. Genetic drift perhaps; the gain
of some inexplicable new feature. None of us knowing
how to fix what we break.

There Were Treats to Be Had

I was trying to make the pieces match. This thing with that.
Not much fit but you can get used to it. The laughing. The
Crying. We comingled in the streets. Nobody too
Obstreperous. All of us agreeing it had gone too long, too far.
Material drifted down through the trees. Confetti, perhaps—
Particulates we couldn't name hung from buildings.
At first no one was too concerned. At first there were
Treats to be had and we were singing the songs.
It was making me anxious though. The tune. The questionable
Blend of happy and sad; those atonal quarter notes, the way
Love sounds when it gets stranded. I apologize for my lack of
Effervescence. We were trying to make the tune attractive.

I didn't see it to begin with though it looks like
Nothing could've prevented it. We sought to
Conceal what went awry when it shifted.
Originally, I was a girl but after that
Never again. Everything seemed gargantuan,
Gorgeous, gratuitous. Reckless, one by one
Raiding each other for ideas, for sex. Perhaps
Ugly about it sometimes—the beds we made
Outfitting ourselves war after war. No
Umpire. No god. No way around it. And yes, we
Saw it. We said something. We were there.

Incubators lined up alongside the walls, the infants
Nodding to themselves behind glass. We tried to
Cauterize the wounds we were making but too much had
Occurred while we were sleeping. We smiled,
Held each other's hands around a circle of flowers trying to
Elicit some comfort in it. The babies were turning on their
Rubbery mattresses. How could it have happened? Who
Emptied out that tank? The spillage. The chairs falling.
Not even the king's men, the babies without names.
Tractors moving back and forth across distant fields.

I didn't see it at first. I was trying to make it make sense. Fish were
Rising out of the rivers and we thought it was the sunset.
All along we were sure about what we were seeing. People were
Singing at the edge of the water when they saw it. Those flashing
Iridescent gills. We thought we had a handle on it. So what if it
Collapsed? Some were laughing and we were being happy.
Bless you, she said to me, *Blessings.* Who could trust it, that
labile god? The laughter. The singing. The fish with their scales.
Eventually I put down the megaphone and walked away.

Yes, it's like in a movie

                              where the villain
refuses to die. Just when you think he's been

extinguished, drowned, fucked beyond
   some super massive black hole

his head and legs start to flail while
his pulsating body is fed and cleared by

offspring. You are of course free to live
   a life of apparent ease but *we've been talking*

in a dream for years. Some nights
   I want to go out and lean my face into

the dark hub of that home carousel of stars
   which I cannot name. How to reconcile

with this thing that should never be
   reconciled with? What crop is that? What

wheat is this in our mouths? Which
flock of birds wheeling through the trees?

Heaven's Breath

This morning the last day of the year
I am thinking about the 30 million
living things balanced on a person's
shoulders in a precarious column 1000
meters high. Don't ask me where
I got that fact but it's a fact and I saw it.
You apparently don't need to worry
about keeping it balanced. Can walk
down the street and keep it all in place.
Can sit in a chair in your living room
with the million or so skin cells you shed
each day and your home filling up with dust.
If you get up and walk down the street, it
goes with you. Like epaulets. Towering
shoulder pads. The thing you can carry
without worry. The day you get up into.
If you turn the right direction in the sunlight
that column might suddenly shine, the
shaft of particles dancing in the beam.
It is not a falling house, this strange science
but we would sincerely like someone
to let us know when the party is over.
And where does that column go when
you die? How to stuff it in a casket.
Into a hole in the ground. Into an urn.
How to set it on fire.

A Common Misperception

It's quiet like that. Bucolic.
Looks like nothing's going wrong anywhere at all.
Bare trees rocking back and forth. Three crows
chasing an owl across the field into the woods.
Yesterday, men appeared at the top of the drive—
rifles, orange vests, big boots, at the same moment
dog ran at them barking and a 350-ton C-5 Air Force
cargo plane grazed us all. Its 200-foot wingspan at treetop,
the noise of it making each of us hold his or her
breath for a moment. Dog didn't bite the men.
Men didn't shoot the dog; plane didn't crash.
Of course they were puzzled by the woman shouting
from the doorway of the house.

*

I wasn't shouting. I was swearing. At my dog. At men
with rifles. Cargo planes. Forest. One week after
San Bernardino. The inexplicable mother and father.
It gets confusing. Which was which. When and where.
Hands up, or down on the ground? On a bike. In a car.
We heard the shots. Saw someone fall. The plane.
Boots on the ground. Dog barking.
One thing blending to another. Linkage disequilibrium, yes.
Something vestigial in us all. You might be the enemy
you were fighting from the air. What you know
might be useful information if you could shake your own self
down. Could remember what country you came from. What
language you were taught to speak. If you were the men
in the plane or the men the plane had come to take.
If you were the plane, or if you were the bolts
on that plane or simply a passenger. What feeds us. What
we feed on. The men faded back into the woods. The plane
disappeared. Dog came back into the house.

When the whales washed

You can be guilty of things you are not guilty of (D.Trump)

into shore because the seals had moved in and following them the great white sharks, we set up our tents on shore. Houses were falling in off the dunes and people came a long way just to see giant living rooms opening up onto the sea, couches, chairs, heirlooms falling out. Some said it was just desserts, taking up all that land. Having that much money. Some said it was the end of the world. The waves at second floor windows. The marble counters going back to the earth out of which they came. There's always someone cheering for the end of it all; the killed dancing with the killers. A shout out to the boss. They've got their bunkers with guns and canned goods. Some reading matter. And out beyond the breakers, the dorsal fins slipping north to south and back again. As if the sharks were reading something to themselves. It's what many of us do. If there's something to read, we read it. The promises on the back of the cereal box. The letters on the wall. The flood levels on the fairground barns. This is how high the river was in 1978. This is how drowned you would have been if you'd been standing here then. Which is why many of us don't stand in one place very long. You keep your feet moving. You know where the hills are. You know how to get there.

Notes

In "Seven Girls Driving Around Town": The first and last line is from Petrarch via a Tupelo Press prompt.

"Yes, it's like in a movie": includes lines from Arthur Miller's *Death of a Salesman*.

ABOUT THE AUTHOR

Carol Potter grew up on a dairy farm in NW Connecticut; she's a Vermont resident, formerly of Los Angeles after years in Western Massachusetts—hence the variety of landscapes and creatures in these pages. Along with the Pacific Coast Poetry Series award from Beyond Baroque, she received a Creation Grant from the Vermont Arts Council in 2019, and was awarded the 2014 FIELD Poetry Prize for her book, *Some Slow Bees,* and the 1998 Cleveland State Poetry Center award as well as The Balcones Award for *Short History of Pets.* Other awards include a Pushcart Award and residencies at Yaddo, MacDowell, The Fundación Valparaíso, and Millay Colony of the Arts. Publications include poems in *The American Poetry Review, Poetry, Green Mountains Review, Hotel Amerika, Sinister Wisdom, The Kenyon Review, Hayden's Ferry Review.* Potter teaches for Antioch University's Low-Residency MFA Program in Los Angeles and she also conducts private poetry workshops. Visit her website at cwpotterverse.com.

ABOUT PACIFIC COAST POETRY SERIES

The Pacific Coast Poetry Series, an imprint of Beyond Baroque Books, was founded by poet Henry Morro in 2013, together with co-editor Suzanne Lummis and associate editor Liz Camfiord.

The Pacific Coast Poetry Series has a special interest in the American West, but is open to poets nationwide. We favor accomplished poetry that's both lucid and smart, poetry that might surprise the reader through its wit or through its depth of feeling.

Our first publication, *Wide Awake: Poets of Los Angeles and Beyond*, was cited by *The Los Angeles Times* as one of the Best Books of 2015. In 2017, we published *Our Foreigner* by the noted Northwest Coast poet, Nance Van Winckel. Molly Bendall, in her review for *Tupelo Quarterly*, praised Van Winckel's "wisecracking and shifty voice," and the way she "holds us captive even as she might unexpectedly jump the tracks."

In 2018, *In Order of Disappearance* by Carine Topal became the third book in the Pacific Coast Poetry Series and was lauded by Dorothy Barresi as a "breathtaking meditation on death, injustice, and the lyric memory's power to name what survives when everything has been stripped away."

Lost and Local by Carol Ellis is Pacific Coast Poetry Series' fourth publication. Of it, David Bespiel wrote, "Carol Ellis' *Lost and Local* possesses a lyrical acuity that is absolving and redemptive."

Pacific Coast Poetry Series would like to thank the Lawrence Lipton Trust for its generous support.

IN MEMORIAM, HENRY J. MORRO (1952 – 2022)

The Pacific Coast Poetry Series will always be grateful to, and will never forget, the founder of this press—that poet brimming with mischief, talent, energy and, sometimes, impassioned opinions, Henry J. Morro. Back in 2013, when he was a Trustee at Beyond Baroque, Henry had the idea to start up a new press. His and his wife Amy's savings made that possible. Along with himself, he perceived in me and Liz Camfiord the skills and experience needed to get such a project off the ground.

What a first year we had. For a while, the press bounced along the ground before it took off. We didn't have a name, much less a first project. Finally, we did—got ourselves a name, got a first project: the anthology *Wide Awake: Poets of Los Angeles and Beyond*, which continues to introduce readers to a couple generations of noted Los Angeles poets.

Henry died this year after the early onset of an age-related illness. I sure miss him, his humor and his fire. His conviction. When Henry J. Morro believed in you, well, you felt *believed in.*

But we have his poems, some damn good ones. I recommend *Zoot Suit Files* (Bambez Press, 2020), poems which Carine Topal and I edited and assembled into a book, and Amy Morro published.

Below is the bio he always used, but such capsulized accounts only hint at a life. If you want to know more, you know where to go. To the poetry.

—Suzanne Lummis

 Henry J. Morro was born in Costa Rica and at the age of two his family moved to San Francisco. He lived there until he was sixteen, when his family reversed the American Dream and moved back to Nicaragua. After the great earthquake in 1972, his family moved to Los Angeles. He graduated from California State University, Los Angles, and began writing poetry. He has taught poetry in public schools and prisons. He has also edited literary journals and anthologies. In addition to his poetry appearing in West Coast and national publications, in 1994 New Alliance Records released *Somoza's Teeth*, a CD recording of his poetry. His new and selected poems, *The Zoot Suit Files*, is available online and at Beyond Baroque. Henry is survived by his wife and two daughters.

SPATS

I snatch a pair of two-toned spats from the thrift store—
cool and out of style in my baggy jeans.

I walk to Macy's and stand in front of the window display
staring at myself in the breeze, my raven hair blowing,

the new mannequins framed into position & the old ones
stripped on the carpet, their gold pumps in a box

beside their heads. Still looking, a crisp wind bites
my ears, my lips crack, but I'm in those beautiful shoes—

a deep brown bordered by a creamy tan. I'm tapping to
the streetcar's night-clanging as it rotates on the platform,

my reflection rising up from the high-tops while I
stand there, aching like a rock star.

— Henry Morro

ABOUT LAWRENCE LIPTON

Lawrence Lipton was born in Poland, 1903, and in the 30s through the 60s established himself as a novelist, journalist and poet, first in Chicago and later in Los Angeles. In Chicago he mingled with the noted writers and literati, Carl Sandburg, Ben Hecht, and Harriet Monroe, editor of the famed literary magazine, *Poetry*.

In addition to his literary novels *Brother, the Laugh is Bitter* and *Secret Battle*, Lipton also wrote mystery novels. His work appeared in newspapers, literary journals and magazines including *The Jewish Daily Forward*, *The Quarterly Review of Literature* and *The Atlantic Monthly*. He published a poetry collection, *Rainbow at Midnight*.

Lipton's *The Holy Barbarians*, published in 1959, explored the impact of the "Beats" upon the society of that day. In his analysis Lipton noted, "When the barbarians appear on the frontiers of a civilization it is a sign of a crisis in that civilization. If the barbarians come, not with weapons of war but with the songs and ikons of peace, it is a sign that the crisis is one of a spiritual nature. In either case the crisis is never welcomed by the entrenched beneficiaries of the status quo. In the case of the holy barbarians it is not an enemy invasion threatening the gates, it is 'a change felt in the rhythm of events' that signals one of those 'cyclic turns' which the poet Robinson Jeffers has written about."

Lipton's son, James Lipton, won wide fame as the executive producer, writer and host of the renowned Bravo series *Inside the Actors Studio*.

Lawrence Lipton died in Los Angeles in 1975. The Lawrence Lipton Trust was created by his widow to support poets.

ABOUT BEYOND BAROQUE BOOKS

The Beyond Baroque Foundation began in 1968 as an avant-garde poetry magazine called *Beyond Baroque*. Editor, publisher and founder George Drury Smith created the Beyond Baroque press in order to publish emerging, over-looked, as well as established, poets— especially those from Los Angeles. The Foundation began issuing perfect-bound books and chapbooks in 1971. Titles include *Building Some Changes*, the first book from Los Angeles' first Poet Laureate, Eloise Klein Healy, Maxine Chernoff's first collection, *Vegetable Emergency* as well as K. Curtis Lyle's *15 Predestination Weather Reports*. Beyond Baroque, through its various publications, also published works by Dennis Cooper, Amy Gerstler, Bill Mohr, Harry Northup, Holly Prado, and Wanda Coleman to name a few. The Foundation's current press, Beyond Baroque Books, was launched in 1998 by Fred Dewey. It has published numerous books and several magazines featuring works by Jean-Luc Godard, Jack Hirschman, Diane di Prima, David Meltzer, Puma Perl and more. Beyond Baroque Books continues to unearth cult rarities as well as collections by noted performance poets, educators, and cultural leaders. Pacific Coast Poetry Series is an imprint of Beyond Baroque Books.

ABOUT BEYOND BAROQUE

Based in the original City Hall building in Venice, California, Beyond Baroque celebrated its 50th anniversary in 2018 as one of the United States' leading independent Literary Arts Centers, dedicated to expanding the public's knowledge of poetry, literature and art through cultural events and community interaction. The building also houses The Mike Kelley Gallery and a bookstore, The Scott Wannberg Bookstore and Poetry Lounge, which stocks an extensive collection of new poetry as well as an archive of more than 40,000 books, including small press and limited-edition publications, chronicling the history of poetry movements in Los Angeles and beyond. Since its founding in 1968 as a magazine by George Drury Smith, BeyondBaroque has played muse to the Venice Beats, the burgeoning Punk movement and visiting scholars.

Beyond Baroque's mission is to advance the literary arts; to provide a challenging program of events which promotes new work and diversity; to foster the exchange of ideas and the nurturing of writers through readings, workshops, books sales, publication, access to archived material and performance space; to encourage collaboration and cross-fertilization between writers and artists in multiple disciplines and to use the literary arts as a foundation for increasing education and literacy in our community and among our youth.

Made in the USA
Middletown, DE
19 May 2022

65922169R00073